THE PHOENIX
AND THE
TORTOISE

KENNETH REXROTH

NEW DIRECTIONS

NORFOLK · CONNECTICUT

For Marie

I would not have you less than mutable,
Leaf wickered sunlight on your lips,
And on your lips the plangent, unstable
Laughter of your copious heart.

CONTENTS

ABOUT THE POEMS

THE poems in this book might be considered as developing, more or less systematically, a definite point of view. That development proceeds genetically or historically. The classical paraphrases come first. They are mostly from Hellenistic, Byzantine and Late Roman sources, and from Martial. I have tended to select those that best show forth a sense of desperation and abandon in the face of a collapsing system of cultural values. In contrast, there are other epigrams of resignation, the famous Clito epitaph for instance.

Other paraphrases occur in the main body of shorter poems. They are put there because they are more freely treated, and because they provide a transition to the main theme of the poems with which they are associated—the discovery of a basis for the recreation of a system of values in sacramental marriage. The process as I see it goes something like this: from abandon to erotic mysticism, from erotic mysticism to the ethical mysticism of sacramental marriage, thence to the realization of the ethical mysticism of universal responsibility—from the Dual to the Other. These poems might well be dedicated to D. H. Lawrence, who died in the attempt to refound a spiritual family. One of the poems is a conscious paraphrase of one of his.

The Phoenix and the Tortoise is an attempt to portray the whole process in historical, personal and physical terms. I have tried to embody in verse the belief that the only valid conservation of value lies in the assumption of unlimited liability, the supernatural identification of the self with the tragic unity of creative process. I hope I have made it clear that I do not believe that the Self does this by an act of Will, by sheer assertion. He who would save his life must lose it.

If the shorter poems might well be dedicated to Lawrence, *The Phoenix and the Tortoise* might well be dedicated to Albert Schweitzer, the man who, in

9

our time, pre-eminently has realized the dream of Leonardo da Vinci. Leonardo died impotent and broken, all his projects half done. He proved that the human will is too small a door for the person to force through into universality. Schweitzer is an outstanding example of a man who found that door which is straight, and smaller than a needle's eye, but through which the universalization of the human soul, the creation of the true person, comes freely, as a guest.

—K. R.

· I ·

THE PHOENIX AND THE TORTOISE

THE PHOENIX AND
THE TORTOISE

I

Webs of misery spread in the brain,
In the dry spring in the soft heat.
Dirty cotton bolls of cloud hang
At the sky's edge; vague yellow stratus
Glimmer behind them. It is storming
Somewhere far out in the ocean.
All night vast rollers exploded
Offshore; now the sea has subsided
To a massive, uneasy torpor.
Fragments of its inexhaustible
Life litter the shingle, sea hares,
Broken starfish, a dead octopus,
And everywhere, swarming like ants,
Innumerable hermit crabs,
Hungry and efficient as maggots.

This is the not the first time this shingle
Has been here. These cobbles are washed
From ancient conglomerate beds,
Beaches of the Franciscan series,
The immense layer cake of grey strata
That hangs without top or bottom
In the geological past
Of the California Coast Ranges.
There are no fossils in them. Their
Dates are disputed—thousands of feet,
Thousands and thousands of years, of bays,
Tidemarshes, estuaries, beaches,
Where time flowed eventless as silt.
Further along the beach the stones
Change; the cliffs are yellow with black
Bands of lignite; and scattered amongst
The sand dollars in the storm's refuse
Are fossil sand dollars the sea
Has washed from stone, as it has washed
These, newly dead, from life.

And I,
Walking by the viscid, menacing
Water, turn with my heavy heart
In my baffled brain, Plutarch's page—
The falling light of the Spartan
Heroes in the late Hellenic dusk—
Agis, Cleomenes—this poem
Of the phoenix and the tortoise—
Of what survives and what perishes,
And how, of the fall of history
And waste of fact—on the crumbling
Edge of a ruined polity
That washes away in an ocean
Whose shores are all washing into death.

A group of terrified children
Has just discovered the body
Of a Japanese sailor bumping
In a snarl of kelp in a tidepool.
While the crowd collects, I stand, mute
As he, watching his smashed ribs breathe
Of the lift of the ocean, his white
Torn bowels braid themselves with the kelp;
And, out of his drained grey flesh, he
Watches me with open hard eyes
Like small indestructible animals—
Me—who stand here on the edge of death,
Seeking the continuity,
The germ plasm, of history,
The epic's lyric absolute.

What happened, and what is remembered—
Or—history is the description
Of those forms of man's activity
Where value survives at the lowest
Level necessary to insure
Temporal continuity.
Or "as the Philosopher says,"
The historian differs from
The poet in this: the historian
Presents what did happen, the poet

What might happen. For this reason
Poetry is more philosophic
Than history, and less trivial.
Poetry presents generalities,
History merely particulars.
So action is generalized
Into what an essential person
Must do by virtue of his essence—
Acting in an imaginary
Order of being, where existence
And essence, as in the Deity
Of Aquinas, fuse in pure act.
What happens in the mere occasion
To human beings is recorded
As an occurence in the gulf
Between essence and existence—
An event of marginal content.

In the artificially bright
Evening of the clocks of war,
In the last passover of the just,
We too prepare symbolic supper.
The low fog coils across the sun,
And falls back, and the powerful
Gold Aten blades of the desert sun
Shine again on the desert land
And over the fog bound ocean.
One side of the canyon is frigid
With shadow, and the other busy
In the dense heat. I build the fire
At the stream's edge. The flames are pale
In the sunlight, thick and fleshy
In their reflections on the water.

While I wait for the water to boil,
I stand, abstract, one breathing man,
On the suture of desert, sea,
And running water brief as spring.
Sagebrush and seaweed, sand and granite,
Mice and plankton, sterile and swarming
Steam and spume, inhale and exhale—

Out of this the ancient Chinese
Built up their whole cosmology—
Rest that dissipates into motion,
And motion that freezes into rest.
And you ride up, hungry, shouting
For supper, on a red stallion,
Breasts quivering in their silk blouse.
Yin and Yang . . . possibly history
Is only an irritability,
A perversion of the blood's chemistry,
The after effects of a six thousand
Year's dead solar cyclone.

                         In the twilight . . .
Here, on the soft unblemished skin,
Where ear and jaw and throat are joined,
Where a flush begins to spread
Under the glittering down;
Here, where the gracious eyebrow
Tapers over the orbit and onto the edge
Of the blue shadowed temple;
Here, on the lips curled back
To begin a smile, showing the teeth
And the tongue tip . . . kisses in the evening,
After supper on the anniversary
Of the white gift of sacramental flesh.

Of what body. Through what years. In what light.

Value and fact are polar aspects
Of organic process. As plus
Is to minus a value: "virtue"
And minus is privative "fact";
So minus is to virtue, "sin."
That is, quality is the aspect
Assumed in perspective of polar
Antitheses of achievement.
How comfortable, and how verbal.

The free laughter and the ivory feet
Treading the grapes—the tousled hair—

The dark juice rising between the thighs
Of the laughing, falling girl, spreading
Through the dark pubic hair, over
The laughing belly.

                         The law by which
We live is the law by which we die.
Again, "as the Philosopher says,"
The ground of individuation
Is the ground of communication.
As pure potentials, the mistresses
Of Alexander and the bedmates
Of the perdurable fellahin
Return finally from history
To the common ground of all discourse.

Found in the smashed tent on Everest—
"Dear Noel,
              We'll probably start
early tomorrow (8th) in order
to have clear weather. It wont be
too early to start looking out
for us either crossing the neckband
under the pyramid or going
up to the skyline at 8 p.m.
yours ever,
              Geo. Mallory"

When process is defined as the field
Suspended between positive
And negative, the Absolute One
And the Absolute Many, the poles
Of being short circuit in reason.
The definition dissolves itself.
Anode and cathode deliquesce
By virtue of inherent structure.
Unavoidably the procedures
Of logic flatter the Deity.

Not want and fear, but the rigid
Vectors of the fallible mind
Confuse all pantheons and haunt

Geometries—and if not fear
And hunger, then danger and desire.
Always the struggle to break out
Of the argument that proves itself,
Past procedure as perimeter,
Past the molecular landslide,
Past the centrifugal perspectives
Of precipitous gain and loss,
Past the attrition of estate . . .
On the frontiers, all boundaries fuse,
Peaks, passes and glaciers, kisses,
Lips and epistemologies.
And the wardens of ontology,
The lethal sophists and policemen,
Patrol the surveyed boundaries.
In the bistros and academies
Rhetoricians seek the absolute
Hallucination. In the bureaux
Of policy it is put in practice.
History is the chronicle
Of the more spectacular failures
To discover vital conflict.

Not want and fear, but danger and desire . . .
Contemporary mysticism
Accounts for all motivation
By the bitch's tit and the dropped pup.
(The vectors don't explain themselves)
Well might the aging precieuse cry out,
"Zénon! Cruel Zénon d'Elée!"
Or turgid Webster lucidly say,
"Like diamonds we are cut with our own dust."

Danger and desire, or jealousy
And fear of pain, the constant pressure
For the lesser, immediate, good . . .
The three tragedians saw lives
As strung on doom, like the lion's teeth
On his still tensile sinews;
Persons as trophies, the savage

Jewelry of continuity
From "pure function to pure potential"
And Karma, the terrifying
Accumulation of bare fact.
And in dynamic antithesis,
The person as priest and victim—
The fulfillment of uniqueness
In perfect identification,
In ideal representation,
As the usurping attorney,
The real and effective surrogate.

Iphigenia at Aulis—
The ritual person emerges
As term of responsibility.
Doom or responsibility—
Fashionable superstition builds
The world from "intervals at which
Accidents are likely to happen."
Catastrophic contingency
In physics or theology,
God as pure fiat, the person
As pure caprice, ends in the worship
Of history as demonic will,
The pandemic destroying Europe.

The lucid Socratic drama
Defines tragedy by example;
Aristotle's recipe book
Neglects to explain why tragedy
Is tragic, the hero, heroic.
Even the Angelic Doctor,
When he came to deal with angels,
That is, personality as such,
Produced the perfect anti-person.
Scotus— Luther— Kierkegaard— Barth—
The dark Gothic demonolatry,
Or the spotless imitation man,
One of David's noble lay figures—

The Oath of the Horatii—
The flesh made of highly polished lead.

The problem of personality
Is the problem of the value
Of the world as a totality,
The problem of immortality
As a basic category—
That passed away, so will this.
The moraine creeps on the meadow;
The temples dissolve in the jungle;
The patterns abide and reassert
Themselves; the texture wears through the nap.

All the terminals coalesce
In the region that defines reason.
In this wilderness as men say
Are the trees of the Sun and the Moon
That spake to King Alexander
And told him of his death.

                        And they took
The head of Bran, and came to Harlech
And the three birds of Rhiannon
Came and sang to them for seven years;
And it seemed as though the birds were far
Distant over the sea, and yet
They were clear, and distinct, and close.
And they went to Gwales in Penvro
To a kingly and spacious hall
That overlooked the sea. And the third
Door that looked towards Cornwall was closed.
And they placed the head in high honor,
And dined and drank and were happy,
And remembered none of their sorrow.
And after fourscore years, on a day,
Heilyn ap Gwynn opened the door
To see if Bran had spoken the truth.
And they looked out over Cornwall
And Aber Henvelen, and as they looked,
They saw all the evils they had suffered,

And all the companions they had lost,
And all the old misery, and the death
Of their good lord, all as though once again,
It was happening there, in that same spot.
And they could not stay, but went to London,
And buried the head in the White Mount.

The perfect circle. The perfect term.

Endurance, novelty, and simple
Occurrence—and here I am, a node
In a context of disasters,
Still struggling with the old question,
Often and elaborately begged.
The atoms of Lucretius still,
Falling, inexplicably swerve.
And the generation that purposed
To control history vanishes
In its own apotheosis
Of calamity, unable
To explain why anything
Should happen at all.

One more spring, and after the bees go,
The soft moths stagger in the firelight;
And silent, vertiginous, sliding,
The great owls hunt low in the air;
And the dwarf owls speak at their burrows.
We walk under setting Orion,
Once more in the dim boom of the sea,
Between bearded, dying apple trees,
In the shadows of the Easter moon;
And silent, vertiginous, the stars
Slide over us past the equinox.
The flowers whirl away in the wind like snow.
The thing that falls away is myself.
The moonlight of the Resurrection,
The moon of Amida on the sea,
Glitters on the wings of the bombers,
Illuminates the darkened cities.
The motion of Egyptian chisels
Dissolves slowly in the desert noon.

It is past midnight and the faint,
Myriad crying of the seabirds
Enters my sleep. The wind rises.
I hear the unbelievably
Distant voices of the multitudes
Of men mewing in the thoroughfares
Of dreams. The waves crowd on the beach.
A log falls in the fire. The wind
Funnels the sparks out in the moonlight
Like a glowing tree dragged through dark.
I see in sudden total vision
The substance of entranc'd Boehme's awe:
The illimitable hour glass
Of the universe eternally
Turning, and the gold sands falling
From God, and the silver sands rising
From God, the double splendors of joy
That fuse and divide again
In the narrow passage of the Cross.

The source of individuation—
The source of communication—
Peace, the conservation of value—
Came Jesus and stood in the midst, and
Saith unto them, "Peace be unto you."
And when he had so said, he shewed
Unto them his hands and his side.

The fire is dense again in the dark.
I turn my face into shadow
And fall again towards sleep,

    Amida,
Kwannon, turn from peace. As moonlight
Flows on the tides, innumerable
Dark worlds flow into splendor.

How many nights have we awakened—
The killdeer crying in the seawind.

II

I am cold in my folded blanket,
Huddled on the ground in the moonlight.

The crickets cry in congealing frost;
Field mice run over my body;
The frost thickens and the night goes by.

North of us lies the vindictive
Foolish city asleep under its guns;
Its rodent ambitions washing out
In sewage and unwholesome dreams.
Behind the backs of drowsy sentries
The moonlight shines through frosted glass—
On the floors of innumerable
Corridors the mystic symbols
Of the bureaucrats are reversed—
Mirrorwise, as Leonardo
Kept the fever charts of one person.
Two Ptahs, two Muhammad's coffins,
We float in the illimitable
Surgery of moonlight, isolate
From each other and the turning earth;
Motionless; frost on our faces;
Eyes by turns alive, dark in the dark.

The State is the organization
Of the evil instincts of mankind.
History is the penalty
We pay for original sin.
In the conflict of appetite
And desire, the person finally
Loses; either the technology
Of the choice of the lesser evil
Overwhelms him; or a universe
Where the stars in their courses move
To ends that justify their means
Dissolves him in its elements.
He cannot win, not on this table.
The World, the Flesh, and the Devil—
The Tempter offered Christ mastery
Of the three master institutions,

God-parents of all destruction—
"Miracle, Mystery, and Authority—"
The systematization of
Appetitive choice to obtain
Desire by accumulation.

History continuously
Bleeds to death through a million secret
Wounds of trivial hunger and fear.
Its stockholders' private disasters
Are amortized in catastrophe.

War is the health of the State? Indeed!
War is the State. All personal
Anti-institutional values
Must be burnt out of each generation.
If a massive continuum
Of personality endured
Into grandchildren, history
Would stop.

       "As the Philosopher says,"
Man is a social animal;
That is, top dog of a slave state.
All those lucid, noble minds admired
Sparta, and well they might. Surely
It is highly questionable
If Plato's thesis can be denied.
The Just Man is the Citizen.
Wars exist to take care of persons.
The species affords no aberrants.

Barmaid of Syria, her hair bound
In a Greek turban, her flanks
Learnedly swaying, shivering
In the shiver of castanets,
Drunk, strutting lasciviously
In the smoke filled tavern . . .

What nexus gathers and dissolves here
In the fortuitous unity
Of revolving night and myself?
They say that history, defining

Responsibility in terms
Of the objective continuum,
Limits, and at the same time creates,
Its participants. They further say
That rational existence is
Essentially harmonic selection.
Discarding "is", the five terms
Are equated, the argument closed.
Cogito and Ergo and Sum play
Leapfrog— fact— process— process —fact—
Between my sleeping body and
The galaxy what Homeric
Heroes struggle for my arms?

Fact and value, process and value,
"Process, not result of judgment,"
Or, result, not process of judgment,
Or, judgment, not result of process,
Or, judgment of result, not process,
The possible combinations
Can be found by arithmetic
Or learned in the School of Experience.
The whalebone sieves the whale food
From the plankton, the plankton
Finally dissolves the whale,
Liberating the whalebone.
Liberty is the mother
Not the daughter of order.

Value evolves in decision;
History passes, pedetemtim;
The results of decision dissolve.
The assumption of history
Is that the primary vehicle
Of social memory is the State.

The nighthawks cry in the saffron
Twilight over the smoky streets
Of Chicago. It is summer.
Victimae paschali, the wise
Jubilant melody of the
Easter Sequence breaks in the Mass.

The song of the monks is like laughter.
It is spring, intense and sunlit.
The field pieces bang on the warped streets
Of Boston. Riots sweep over the world.
Midsummer—the harvest over.
The American polity
Discards its chrysalis of myth.
Ribbentrop and Stalin exchange smirks,
The fruit falls from the tree. Summer ends.

Was it Carnot who said, "The end
Justifies the means?" Or was it Marx?
Or Adams? "As teleology
Subsides to a minimum, achievement
Rises to a maximum." "The sum
Of conflagration is tepidity."
The infinitely cool, Virgin
Or Dynamo; the term: entropy
Or fecundity; the bleak Yankee
Purposiveness always gnawing:
"You have nothing to lose but your chains."
They are willing to pay any price.
They can be bought for any price.

As the Philosopher says,
That only is natural which contains
The principle of its own change within
Itself; what comes by chance is accident.
Being is statistical likelihood;
Actuaries conjure the actual.
In the words of the Stagirite,
"Nature comes apart at the joints."
Or, a theory of history,
"Physiologists and physicians
Have a fuller knowledge of the human
Body than the most anxious mother."

"The inhabitants of the world
At each successive period
In its history have beaten
Their predecessors in the race
For life, and are, in so far, higher

In the scale." So Darwin himself.
Natura non facit saltum.
The Franciscan series under me
Revolves with the planet, a mile thick
Mummy of blank catastrophe.

Gilbert White in his garden, Darwin
Poking around on the Beagle,
Franklin vanishing in the Arctic,
"There is no such thing as negative
Historical evidence."

The vast onion of the actual:
The universe, the galaxy,
The solar system, and the earth,
And life, and human life, and men's
Relationships, and men, and each man . . .
History seeping from capsule
To capsule, from periphery
To center, and outward again . . .
The sparkling quanta of events,
The pulsing wave motion of value . . .

Marx. Kropotkin. Adams. Acton.
Spengler. Toynbee. Tarn building empires
From a few coins found in a cellar . . .
History . . . the price we pay for man's
First disobedience . . . John of Patmos,
The philosopher of history.

This body huddled on the whirling
Earth, dipping the surface of sleep
As damsel flies sting the water's skin
With life. What is half remembered
In the hypnogogy of time;
Ineradicable bits of tune;
Nicias in rout from Syracuse;
Scarlet Wolsey splendid on the Field
Of the Cloth of Gold; More on trial;
Abelard crying for that girl;
"More than my brother, Jonathan,

27

Of one soul with me,
What sin, what pollution,
Has torn our bowels assunder."
The burnt out watch fires of Modena;
Or Phoebi claro—love, dawn, and fear
Of treacherous death; the enervated
Musical, dim edge of sleep;
Archdeacon Stuck on McKinley
Singing, "Te Deum laudamus . . ."
In the clenching cold and the thin air;
Lawrence dying of his body,
Blue gentians burning in the dark mind;
The conflict of events and change.

In their hour the constellations
Of autumn mount guard over me—
Aquarius and Capricorn,
Watchers of my birth and of the turn
Of the apocalyptic future;
Noah and Pan in deadly conflict,
Watched by Fomalhaut's cold, single eye.
These are the stars that marched over
Boethius in meditation,
Waiting the pleasure of the Goth;
And once Chinese philosophers
Saw all the visible planets
In conjunction in Capricorn,
Two thousand, four hundred, forty-nine
Years before Christ.

        The thinne fame
Yit lasting, of hir ydel names,
Is marked with a fewe lettres . . .

Loken up-on the brode shewinge
Contrees of hevene, and up-on
The streit site of this erthe . . .

Liggeth thanne stille, all outrely
Unknowable; ne fame maketh yow
Not know.

III

Softly and singly an owl
Cries in my sleep. I awake and turn
My head, but there is only the moon
Sinking in the early dawn.
Owls do not cry over the ocean.
The night patrol planes return
Opaque against the transparent moon.
"The owl of Minerva," says Hegel,
"Takes her flight in the evening."
It is terrible to lie
Beside my wife's canvas chrysalis,
Watching the imperceptible
Preparation of morning,
And think that this probably is not
The historical evening we thought;
Waking in the twilight like bemused
Drunkards; but the malignant
Dawn of the literate insect,
Dispassionate, efficient, formic.

Irrelevant appetite dissolves
The neurones of a deranged nation—
Nucleus of alcohol, fibres
"Meandering in pellucid gold."
Remorse and guilt stiffen the tissues
With hypnotic dread of penitence.
Stone lodges against the heart
A blank total of catastrophe—
The bloody heart, suspicious
And ruined, but still the irritant
In the vitals of this iron mollusc,
Still the cause of its daily
Frightened secretions of mud.

The ant has perfect statistical
Intelligence, "a thoroughly
Humean approach to the problem
Of causality." History starts
With the dislocation of units,
The creation of persons,

A phenomenon of diffusion
In the high tension gap between
Technology and environment.
On the edges of riparian
Egypt and Mesopotamia
The dense family societal body
Acquired leucocytes within
And parasites without. "History
Is the instability
Of the family constellation."
Its goal is the achievement
Of the completely atomic
Individual and the pure
Commodity relationship—
The windowless monad sustained
By Providence. History
Ceases in a change of phase—
The polarization of its parts
In a supernatural kindred.

Shogun or Mikado—the Sun King
Eighteen centuries before Christ
Or after—amateur lockmakers
With pussy mistresses—the pure form
Of the cutting edge of power—
Man reduced to an entelechy—
"I lay down my pen in horror,
Not at the thought of Ivan's
Atrocities, but at the thought
That high minded, noble men
For years found it expedient
To bow to his will, to act
As instruments of his monstrous crimes."
"Politics is the art of choosing
The lesser evil." "The State, that's me."
Splendid as a rococo
Sunburst, with its powdered face buried
In the immortal buttocks
Of little Murphy. St. Thomas More
Or venereal Anne Boleyn—
Posterity in gratuity

Has provided both with beautiful
Apocryphal testaments.

The flow of interoffice
Memoranda charts the excretions
Of societal process,
The cast snake skin, the fleeting
Quantum, Economic Man.
Novelty comes to be considered
The unpredictable, process
The clean columbarium
Of consumed statistical
Probabilities. Pascal
Merges with Hume; the stresses
Of the architecture are computed
By roulette; "the foundations
Are ingeniously supported
By the superstructure"; the agent
For insurance evicts that agent
Once thought more noble than the patient,
And his ontology along with him.
In the words of the Philosopher
King, Faustina's husband, "If I don't,
Somebody else will. Think of the good
I can do with my authority."
John Maynard Keynes visits the White House.

"Salvation equals autonomy."
All major religions have said so,
Whatever their founders thought.
Six thousand years of struggle
For autonomy, and what's to pay?
The terrified Phi Beta Kappas
Cower behind the columns
They afforded the masses
Whispering, "E pluribus unum."
Or the Sufi, shrouded in white wool,
Meditating in dead Ctesiphon,
Spinning the erotic metaphors
Of self abandonment—wine, rubies
And perfumed buttocks—for the jackals

And cactus—the slow self destruction
Of the human, consumed away
By the inaccessible sun
Of absolute unity.

Hippias and Socrates
Contending for the title
Of Most Autonomous Greek.
Hippias who duplicated
The cube; who came to Olympia
With all that he had about
His body the work of his own hands—
A ring and seal, a strigil
And vanity case, high shoes and cloak,
And underwear, and a belt,
A perfect imitation
Of the finest Persian leather work;
Who came to Olympia
Carrying tragedies, dithyrambs,
Epics, learned treatises,
And all of his own composition,
Rhetorically sublime,
Grammatically immaculate,
Besides a system of mnemonics;
Who stood in public in all
The Greek cities and had an answer
For all questions; who came to Sparta
With a theory of the Beautiful
All his own, and many ingenious
Contrivances in mathematics,
And found a people interested
Only in archeology
And history—their own history
And the ruins they had made elsewhere.
And Socrates, playing practical
Jokes on the imperium.
As the Philosopher says,
"All men desire to know." A highly
Undetermined appetite.

Atomization versus
Autonomy—the odds are with

The side with the most matériel.
The most resistant elements break
Under sixty centuries
Of attrition; only a species
Of hysteresis preserves
A sort of residue, overplus
Of past renunciation.
The saint becomes a madman,
The sage a crank, the beggar
A pauper, the courtesan
A whore or enthusiast.
Time's crystals lodge against the bitter
Heart at last, even the perfected
Heart of flesh.

                    Eva and Ave,
The swords of history—jealousy,
The fear of autonomous action,
The sharer of the gaudy apple
Of Atalanta and Paris,
Persephone's parchment red
Globule and its carbon chromosomes,
The germ of gold and the counter-heart;
And conversely, the hari-kiri
Sword of history, the goal
Of pure undetermined fiat,
Duns Scotus' Immaculate Virgin,
The sentimental climax
Of aged Goethe's vision,
"The form of the cutting edge—"
And as contradictory, Murphy
Cuddling that sword in tickles,
And lovely bemused Lesbia
Kneeling in every Roman alley.

And somewhere the irreducible
Fused unity and duality,
The fluent, liquid source of number.
The busy Myrmidons, those sly men,
Retreat to the last river,
The continuity of the germ plasm,

The animal tribute to a brief
Eternity. The Philosopher,
"Matter is the tendency
To immediate ends. An exact
And adequate material force
Must always deflect another force.
As the new form evolves, the prior
Recedes reciprocally into
Pure potentiality."

The institution is a device
For providing molecular
Process with delusive credentials.
"Value is the reflection
Of satisfied appetite,
The formal aspect of the tension
Generated by resolution
Of fact." Overspecialization,
Proliferation, gigantism.

Would it have been better to have slept
And dreamed, than to have watched night
Pass and this slow moon sink? My wife sleeps
And her dreams measure the hours
As accurately as my
Meditations in cold solitude.
I have lain awake while the moon crossed,
Dragging at the tangled ways
Of the sea and the tangled, blood filled
Veins of sleepers. I am not alone,
Caught in the turning of the seasons.
As the long beams of the setting moon
Move against the breaking day,
The suspended light pulsates
Like floating snow. Involuntary,
I may live on, sustained in the web
Of accident, never forgetting
This midnight moon that already blurs
In memory.
                As certain
As color passes from the petal,
Irrevocable as flesh,

The gazing eye falls through the world.
As the light breaks over the water
One by one, pedetemtim,
The stakes of the nets appear
Stretching far out into the shallows,
And beyond them the dark animal
Shadow of a camouflaged cruiser.

IV

Dark within dark I cling to sleep,
The heart's capsule closed in the fist
Of circumstance; prison within
Prison, inseparably dark,
I struggle to hold oblivion
As Jacob struggled in a dream,
And woke touched and with another name.
And on the thin brain pan of sleep
The mill of Gaza grinds;
The heart condenses; and beyond
The world's lip the sun to me is dark
And silent as the moon that falls
Through the last degrees of night into
The unknown antipodes. I lie
At random, carelessly diffused,
Stone and amoeba on the verge
Of partition; and beyond the reach
Of my drowsy integrity,
The race of glory and the race
Of shame, just or unjust, alike
Miserable, both come to evil end.

Eventually history
Distills off all accumulated
Values but one. Babies are more
Durable than monuments, the rose
Outlives Ausonius, Ronsard
And Waller, and Horace's pear tree
His immortal column. Once more
Process is precipitated
In the tirelessly receptive womb.
In the decay of the sufficient
Reasonableness of sacraments
Marriage holds by its bona fides.

Beneath what shield and from what flame.

The darkness gathers about Lawrence
Dying by the dead Mediterranean—
Catullus is psychoanalyzed

Between wars in lickerish London.
Another aging precieuse
Drinks cognac, dreams of rutting children
In the Mississippi valley,
Watches the Will destroy the logic
Of Christopher Wren and Richelieu.
Schweitzer plays Bach in the jungle.
It is all over—just and unjust.
The seed leaks through the gravel.

The light grows stronger and my lids
That were black turn red; the blood turns
To the coming sun. I sit up
And look out over the bright quiet
Sea and the blue and yellow cliffs
And the pure white tatters of fog
Dissolving on the black fir ridges.
The world is immovable
And immaculate. The argument
Has come to an end; it is morning,
And in the isolating morning
The problem hangs suspended, lucid
In a crystal cabinet of air
And angels where only bird song wakes.

"Value is the elastic ether
Of quality that fills up the gaps
In the continuum of discreet
Quantity—the prime togetherness."
The assumption of order,
The principle of parsimony,
Remain mysteries; fact and logic
Meet only in catastrophe.
So long ago they discovered that
Each new irrational is the start
Of a new series of numbers;
Called God the source of systematic
Irrationalization of given
Order—the organism that
Geometricizes. And that vain
Boy, systematically deranging
Himself amongst the smoky cannoneers

Of the Commune, finding a bronze
Apotheosis as the perfect
Provincial French merchant who made good.
The statistical likelihood
Of being blown to pieces.

"Value is the reflection
Of satisfied appetite."
The State organizes ecstacy.
The dinosaur wallows in the chilling
Marsh. The bombs fall on the packed dance halls.
The sperm seeks the egg in the gravel.
"Novelty is, by definition,
Value-positive."

   "Value
Is a phase change in the relations
Of events." Does that mean anything?

Morning. It is Good Friday Morning;
Communion has past to Agony
And Agony is gone and only
Responsibility remains; doom
Watches with its inorganic eyes,
The bright, blind regiments, hidden
By the sun-flushed sky, the remote
Indestructible animals.

Value, causality, being,
Are reducible to the purest
Act, the self-determining person,
He who discriminates structure
In contingency, he who assumes
All the responsibility
Of ordered, focused, potential—
Sustained by all the universe,
Focusing the universe in act—
The person, the absolute price,
The only blood defiance of doom.

Whymper, coming down the Matterhorn,
After the mountain had collected
Its terrible, casual fee,

The blackmail of an imbecile beauty:
"About 6 PM we arrived
Upon the ridge descending towards
Zermatt, and all peril was over.
We frequently looked, but in vain,
For traces of our unfortunate
Companions; we bent over the ridge
And cried to them, but no sound returned.
Convinced at last that they were neither
Within sight nor hearing we ceased;
And, too cast down for speech, silently
Gathered up our things and the little
Effects of those who were lost
And prepared to continue
The descent. When, lo! a mighty arch
And beneath it a huge cross of light
Appeared, rising above the Lyskamm
High into the sky. Pale, colorless,
And noiseless, but perfectly sharp
And defined, except where it was lost
In the clouds, this unearthly
Apparition seemed like a vision
From another world; and appalled,
We watched with amazement the gradual
Development of two vast crosses
One on either side . . . Our movements
Had no effect on it, the spectral
Forms remained motionless. It was
A fearful and wonderful sight;
Unique in my experience,
And impressive beyond description,
Coming at such a moment."

Nude, my feet in the cold shallows,
The motion of the water surface
Barely perceptible, and the sand
Of the bottom in fine sharp ridges
Under my toes, I wade out, waist deep
And swim seaward down the narrow inlet.
In the distance, beyond the sand bar,
The combers are breaking, and nearer,

39

Like a wave crest escaped and frozen,
One white egret guards the harbor mouth.
The immense stellar phenomenon
Of dawn focuses in the egret
And flows out, and focuses in me
And flows infinitely away
To touch the last galactic dust.

This is the prime reality—
Bird and man, the individual
Discriminate, the self evalued
Actual, the operation
Of infinite, ordered potential.
Birds, sand grains and souls bleed into being;
The past reclaims its own, "I should have,
I could have—It might have been different—"
Sunsets on Saturn, desert roses,
Corruptions of the will, quality—
The determinable future, fall
Into quantity, into the
Irreparable past, history's
Cruel irresponsiblity.

This is the minimum negative
Condition, the "Condition Humaine,"
The tragic loss of value into
Barren novelty, the condition
Of salvation; out of this alone
The person emerges as complete
Responsible act—this lost
And that conserved—the appalling
Decision of the verb "to be."
Men drop dead in the ancient rubbish
Of the Acropolis, scholars fall
Into self-dug graves, Jews are smashed
Like heroic vermin in the Polish winter.
This is my fault, the horrible term
Of weakness, evasion, indulgence,
The total of my petty fault—
No other man's.

And out of this
Shall I reclaim beauty, peace of soul,
The perfect gift of self-sacrifice
Myself as act, as immortal person?

I walk back along the sandspit,
The horizon cuts the moon in half,
And far out at sea a path of light,
Violent and brilliant, reflected
From high stratus clouds and then again
On the moving sea, the invisible
Sunrise spreads its light before the moon.

My wife has been swimming in the breakers,
She comes up the beach to meet me, nude,
Sparkling with water, singing high and clear
Against the surf. The sun crosses
The hills and fills her hair, as it lights
The moon and glorifies the sea
And deep in the empty mountains melts
The snow of winter and the glaciers
Of ten thousand thousand years.

·II·
SHORTER POEMS

I

"... about the cool water
the wind sounds through sprays
of apple, and from the quivering leaves
slumber pours down ..."

We lie here in the bee filled, ruinous
Orchard of a decayed New England farm,
Summer in our hair, and the smell
Of summer in our twined bodies,
Summer in our mouths, and summer
In the luminous, fragmentary words
Of this dead Greek woman.
Stop reading. Lean back. Give me your mouth.
Your grace is as beautiful as sleep.
You move against me like a wave
That moves in sleep.
Your body spreads across my brain
Like a bird filled summer;
Not like a body, not like a separate thing,
But like a nimbus that hovers
Over every other thing in all the world.
Lean back. You are beautiful,
As beautiful as the folding
Of your hands in sleep.

We have grown old in the afternoon.
Here in our orchard we are as old
As she is now, wherever dissipate
In that distant sea her gleaming dust
Flashes in the wave crest
Or stains the murex shell.
All about us the old farm subsides
Into the honey bearing chaos of high summer.
In those far islands the temples
Have fallen away, and the marble
Is the color of wild honey.
There is nothing left of the gardens
That were once about them, of the fat
Turf marked with cloven hooves.

45

Only the sea grass struggles
Over the crumbled stone,
Over the splintered steps,
Only the blue and yellow
Of the sea, and the cliffs
Red in the distance across the bay.
Lean back.
Her memory has passed to our lips now.
Our kisses fall through summer's chaos
In our own breasts and thighs.

Gold colossal domes of cumulus cloud
Lift over the undulant, sibilant forest.
The air presses against the earth.
Thunder breaks over the mountains.
Far off, over the Adirondacks,
Lightning quivers, almost invisible
In the bright sky, violet against
The grey, deep shadows of the bellied clouds.
The sweet virile hair of thunder storms
Brushes over the swelling horizon.
Take off your shoes and stockings.
I will kiss your sweet legs and feet
As they lie half buried in the tangle
Of rank scented midsummer flowers.
Take off your clothes. I will press
Your summer honeyed flesh into the hot
Soil, into the crushed, acrid herbage
Of midsummer. Let your body sink
Like honey through the hot
Granular fingers of summer.

Rest. Wait. We have enough for a while.
Kiss me with your mouth
Wet and ragged, your mouth that tastes
Of my own flesh. Read to me again
The twisting music of that language
That is of all others, itself a work of art.
Read again those isolate, poignant words
Saved by ancient grammarians
To illustrate the conjugations

And declensions of the more ancient dead.
Lean back in the curve of my body,
Press your bruised shoulders against
The damp hair of my body.
Kiss me again. Think, sweet linguist,
In this world the ablative is impossible.
No other one will help us here.
We must help ourselves to each other.
The wind walks slowly away from the storm;
Veers on the wooded crests; sounds
In the valleys. Here we are isolate,
One with the other; and beyond
This orchard lies isolation,
The isolation of all the world.
Never let anything intrude
On the isolation of this day,
These words, isolate on dead tongues,
This orchard, hidden from fact and history,
These shadows, blended in the summer light,
Together isolate beyond the world's reciprocity.

Do not talk any more. Do not speak.
Do not break silence until
We are weary of each other.
Let our fingers run like steel
Carving the contours of our bodies' gold.
Do not speak. My face sinks
In the clotted summer of your hair.
The sound of the bees stops.
Stillness falls like a cloud.
Be still. Let your body fall away
Into the awe filled silence
Of the fulfilled summer—
Back, back, infinitely away—
Our lips weak, faint with stillness.

See. The sun has fallen away.
Now there are amber
Long lights on the shattered
Boles of the ancient apple trees.
Our bodies move to each other

As bodies move in sleep;
At once filled and exhausted,
As the summer moves to autumn,
As we, with Sappho, move towards death.
My eyelids sink toward sleep in the hot
Autumn of your uncoiled hair.
Your body moves in my arms
On the verge of sleep;
And it is as though I held
In my arms the bird filled
Evening sky of summer.

II

Our canoe idles in the idling current
Of the tree and vine and rush enclosed
Backwater of a torpid midwestern stream;
Revolves slowly, and lodges in the glutted
Waterlilies. We are tired of paddling.
All afternoon we have climbed the weak current,
Up dim meanders, through woods and pastures,
Past muddy fords where the strong smell of cattle
Lay thick across the water; singing the songs
Of perfect, habitual motion; ski songs,
Nightherding songs, songs of the capstan walk,
The levee, and the roll of the voyageurs.
Tired of motion, of the rhythms of motion,
Tired of the sweet play of our interwoven strength,
We lie in each other's arms and let the palps
Of waterlily leaf and petal hold back
All motion in the heat thickened, drowsing air.
Sing to me softly, Westron Wynde, Ah the Syghes,
Mon Coeur se Recommend à Vous, Phoebi Claro;
Sing the wandering erotic melodies
Of men and women gone seven hundred years,
Softly, your mouth close to my cheek.
Let our thighs lie entangled on the cushions,
Let your breasts in their thin cover
Hang pendant against my naked arms and throat;
Let your odorous hair fall across our eyes;
Kiss me with those subtle, melodic lips.
As I undress you, your pupils are black, wet,
Immense, and your skin ivory and humid.
Move softly, move hardly at all, part your thighs,
Take me slowly while our gnawing lips
Fumble against the humming blood in our throats.
Move softly, do not move at all, but hold me,
Deep, still, deep within you, while time slides away,
As this river slides beyond this lily bed,
And the thieving moments fuse and disappear
In our mortal, timeless flesh.

Solitude closes down around us
As we lie passive and exhausted

Solitude clamps us softly in its warm hand.
A turtle slips into the water
With a faint noise like a breaking bubble;
There is no other sound, only the dim
Momentous conversation of windless
Poplar and sycamore leaves and rarely,
A single, questioning frog voice.
I turn my eyes from your entranced face
And watch the oncoming sunset
Powder the immense, unblemished zenith
With almost imperceptible sparkles of gold.
Your eyes open, your head turns.
Your lips nibble at my shoulder.
I feel a languid shudder run over your body.
Suddenly you laugh, like a pure
Exulting flute, spring to your feet
And plunge into the water.
A white bird breaks from the rushes
And flies away, and the boat rocks
Drunkenly in the billows
Of your nude jubilation.

III

The earth will be going on a long time
Before it finally freezes;
Men will be on it; they will take names,
Give their deeds reasons.
We will be here only
As chemical constituents—
A small franchise indeed.
Right now we have lives,
Corpuscles, ambitions, caresses,
Like everybody had once—
All the bright neige d'antan people,
"Blithe Helen, white Iope, and the rest,"
All the uneasy, remembered dead.

Here at the year's end, at the feast
Of birth, let us bring to each other
The gifts brought once west through deserts—
The precious metal of our mingled hair,
The frankincense of enraptured arms and legs,
The myrrh of desperate, invincible kisses—
Let us celebrate the daily
Recurrent nativity of love,
The endless epiphany of our fluent selves,
While the earth rolls away under us
Into unknown snows and summers,
Into untraveled spaces of the stars.

IV

ANOTHER SPRING

The seasons revolve and the years change
With no assistance or supervision.
The moon, without taking thought,
Moves in its cycle, full, crescent, and full.

The white moon enters the heart of the river;
The air is drugged with azalea blossoms;
Deep in the night a pine cone falls;
Our campfire dies out in the empty mountains.

The sharp stars flicker in the tremulous branches;
The lake is black, bottomless in the crystalline night;
High in the sky the Northern Crown
Is cut in half by the dim summit of a snow peak.

O heart, heart, so singularly
Intransigent and corruptible,
Here we lie entranced by the starlit water,
And moments that should each last forever

Slide unconsciously by us like water.

V

Now, on this day of the first hundred flowers,
Fate pauses for us in imagination,
As it shall not ever in reality—
As these swifts that link endless parabolas
Change guard unseen in their secret crevices.
Other anniversaries that we have walked
Along this hillcrest through the black fir forest,
Past the abandoned farm, have been just the same—
Even the fog necklaces on the fencewires
Seem to have gained or lost hardly a jewel;
The annual and diurnal patterns hold.
Even the attrition of the cypress grove
Is slow and orderly, each year one more tree
Breaks ranks and lies down, decrepit in the wind.
Each year, on summer's first luminous morning,
The swallows come back, whispering and weaving
Figure eights around the sharp curves of the swifts,
Plaiting together the summer air all day,
That the bats and owls unravel in the nights.
And we come back, the signs of time upon us,
In the pause of fate, the threading of the year.

VI

There are sparkles of rain on the bright
Hair over your forehead;
Your eyes are wet and your lips
Wet and cold, your cheek rigid with cold.
Why have you stayed
Away so long, why have you only
Come to me late at night
After walking for hours in wind and rain?
Take off your dress and stockings;
Sit in the deep chair before the fire.
I will warm your feet in my hands;
I will warm your breasts and thighs with kisses.
I wish I could build a fire
In you that would never go out.
I wish I could be sure that deep in you
Was a magnet to draw you always home.

VII

MARTIAL — XII, LII

This is your own lover, Kenneth, Maria,
Who someday will be part of the earth
Beneath your feet; who crowned you once with roses
Of song; whose voice was no less famous
Raised against the guilt of his generation.
Sweetly in Hell he'll tell your story
To the enraptured ears of Helen,
Our joys and jealousies, our quarrels and journeys,
That unlike hers, ended in kisses.
Her spouse will smile at impetuous Paris
When he hears the tale of our sweet lust.
Laura and Petrarca, Waller and his Rose,
Grim Dante and glowing Beatrice,
Catullus and Lesbia, and all the rest,
Transparent hand in hand, will listen,
A tremor on their shadowy flesh once more.
And when at last I welcome you there
Your name will stand for memory of living
On the tongues of all whom death has joined.
You shall know this when you see my grave snowless
Winter long, and my cold sleepfellows
Shifting themselves underground to warm
Dead bones at my still glowing ashes.

VIII

THE ADVANTAGES OF LEARNING

I am a man with no ambitions
And few friends, wholly incapable
Of making a living, growing no
Younger, fugitive from some just doom.
Lonely, ill-clothed, what does it matter?
At midnight I make myself a jug
Of hot white wine and cardamon seeds.
In a torn grey robe and old beret,
I sit in the cold writing poems,
Drawing nudes on the crooked margins,
Copulating with sixteen year old
Nymphomaniacs of my imagination.

IX

PRECESSION OF THE EQUINOXES

Time was, I walked in February rain,
My head full of its own rhythms like a shell,
And came home at night to write of love and death,
High philosophy, and brotherhood of man.

After intimate acquaintance with these things,
I contemplate the changes of the weather,
Flowers, birds, rabbits, mice and other small deer
Fulfilling the year's periodicity.

And the reassurances of my own pulse.

X

INVERSELY, AS THE SQUARE OF THEIR DISTANCES APART

It is impossible to see anything
In this dark; but I know this is me, Rexroth,
Plunging through the night on a chilling planet.
It is warm and busy in this vegetable
Darkness where invisible deer feed quietly.
The sky is warm and heavy, even the trees
Over my head cannot be distinguished,
But I know they are knobcone pines, that their cones
Endure unopened on the branches, at last
To grow imbedded in the wood, waiting for fire
To open them and reseed the burned forest.
And I am waiting, alone, in the mountains,
In the forest, in the darkness, and the world
Falls swiftly on its measured ellipse.

XI

It is warm tonight and very still.
The stars are hazy and the river—
Vague and monstrous under the fireflies—
Is hardly audible, resonant
And profound at the edge of hearing.
I can just see your eyes and wet lips.
Invisible, solemn, and fragrant,
Your flesh opens to me in secret.
We shall know no further enigma.
After all the years there is nothing
Stranger than this. We who know ourselves
As one doubled thing, and move our limbs
As deft implements of one fused lust,
Are mysteries in each other's arms.

XII

At the wood's edge in the moonlight
We dropped our clothes and stood naked,
Swaying, shadow mottled, enclosed
In each other and together
Closed in the night. We did not hear
The whip-poor-will, nor the aspen's
Whisper; the owl flew silently
Or cried out loud, we did not know.
We could not hear beyond the heart.
We could not see the moving dark
And light, the stars that stood or moved,
The stars that fell. Did they all fall
We had not known. We were falling
Like meteors, dark through black cold
Toward each other, and then compact,
Blazing through air into the earth.

XIII

I lie alone in an alien
Bed in a strange house and morning
More cruel than any midnight
Pours its brightness through the window—
Cherry branches with the flowers
Fading, and behind them the gold
Stately baubles of the maple,
And behind them the pure immense
April sky and a white frayed cloud,
And in and behind everything,
The inescapable vacant
Distance of loneliness.

XIV

HABEAS CORPUS

You have the body, blood and bone,
And hair and nail and tooth and eye.
You have the body—the skin taut
In the moonlight, the sea gnawing
At the empty mountains, the hair
Of the body tensile, erect ...
The full barley ears whip and flail
In the rain gorged wind and the flame
Of lightning breaks in the air
For a moment and vanishes;
And I tell you the memory
Of flesh is as real as live flesh
Or falling stone or burning fire ...
You have the body and the sun
Brocaded brown and pink naked
Wedded body, its eternal
Blood biding the worm and his time.

XV

PLINY — IX, XXXVI —
LAMPRIDIUS — XXIX

When I remember that letter of Pliny's—
The daily round of a gentleman
Of letters in the days of Trajan—
Masseuses of assorted colors
Before breakfast, all of them learned
In the Greek poets, philosophic
Discourses in the bath, flute players
For lunch, along with mathematics,
Roast peacocks for dinner, and after,
Mixed maenads, or else astronomy,
Depending on the mood and weather—
I am overcome with amazement.
Here I sit, poor, proud, and domestic,
Manipulating my typewriter;
And beyond my library window,
Inordinately luxuriant,
Suffused with esoteric giggles,
The remote daughters of my neighbors
Return from high school.

XVI

Strong ankled, sun burned, almost naked,
The daughters of California
Educate reluctant humanists;
Drive into their skulls with tennis balls
The unhappy realization
That nature is still stronger than man.
The special Hellenic privilege
Of the special intellect seeps out
At last in this irrigated soil.
Sweat of athletes and juice of lovers
Are stronger than Socrates' hemlock;
And the games of scrupulous Euclid
Vanish in the gymnopedia.

XVII

Here I sit, reading the Stoic
Latin of Tacitus.
Tiberius sinks in senile
Gloom as Aeneas sank
In the smoky throat of Hades;
And the prose glitters like
A tray of dental instruments.
The toss head president,
Deep in his private catacomb,
Is preparing to pull
The trigger. His secretaries
Make speeches. In ten years
The art of communication
Will be more limited.
The wheel, the lever, the incline,
May survive, and perhaps,
The alphabet. At the moment
The intellectual
Advance guard is agitated
Over the relation
Between the Accumulation
Of Capital and the
Systematic Derangement of
The Senses, and the Right
To Homosexuality.

XVIII

Remember that breakfast one November—
Cold black grapes smelling faintly
Of the cork they were packed in,
Hard rolls with hot, white flesh,
And thick, honey sweetened chocolate?
And the parties at night; the gin and the tangos?
The torn hair nets, the lost cuff links?
Where have they all gone to,
The beautiful girls, the abandoned hours?
They said we were lost, mad and immoral,
And interfered with the plans of the management.
And today, millions and millions, shut alive
In the coffins of circumstance,
Beat on the buried lids,
Huddle in the cellars of ruins, and quarrel
Over their own fragmented flesh.

XIX

3 A.M., the night is absolutely still;
Snow squeals beneath my skis, plumes on the turns.
I stop at the canyon's edge, stand looking out
Over the Great Valley, over the millions—
In bed, drunk, loving, tending mills, furnaces,
Alone, wakeful, as the world rolls in chaos.
The quarter moon rises in the black heavens—
Over the sharp constellations of the cities
The cold lies, crystalline and silent,
Locked between the mountains.

XX

Irresolute, pausing on a doubtful journey;
Once more, after so long, the unique autumnal
Wonder of the upper Hudson about me;
I walk in the long forgotten
Familiar garden. The house was never
Reoccupied, the windows are broken,
The walks and the arbors ruinous,
The flower beds are thickets,
The hedges are shattered,
The quince and hawthorns broken and dying.
One by one the memories of twenty years
Vanish and there is no trace of them.
I have been restless in many places
Since I rested in this place.
The dry thickets are full of migrating
Grey green warblers. Since last fall
They have visited Guatemala and Labrador
And now they are bound south again.
Their remote ancestors were doing the same thing
When I was here before. Each generation
Has stopped for an autumn evening
Here, in this place, each year.

XXI

DELIA REXROTH

Died June, 1916

Under your illkempt yellow roses,
Delia, today you are younger
Than your son. Two and a half decades—
The family monument sagged askew,
And he overtook your half-a-life.
On the other side of the country,
Near the willows by the slow river,
Deep in the earth, the white ribs retain
The curve of your fervent, careful breast;
The fine skull, the ardor of your brain.
And in the fingers the memory
Of Chopin études, and in the feet
Slow waltzes and champagne twosteps sleep.
And the white full moon of midsummer,
That you watched awake all that last night,
Watches history fill the deserts
And oceans with corpses once again;
And looks in the east window at me,
As I move past you to middle age
And knowledge past your agony and waste.

XXII

ANDREE REXROTH

Died October, 1940

Now once more grey mottled buckeye branches
Explode their emerald stars,
And alders smoulder in a rosy smoke
Of innumerable buds.
I know that spring again is splendid
As ever, the hidden thrush
As sweetly tongued, the sun as vital—
But these are the forest trails we walked together,
These paths, ten years together.
We thought the years would last forever,
They are all gone now, the days
We thought would not come for us are here.
Bright trout poised in the current—
The racoon's track at the water's edge—
A bittern booming in the distance—
Your ashes scattered on this mountain—
Moving seaward on this stream.

XXIII

AGAIN AT WALDHEIM

> "Light upon Waldheim"
> —*Voltairine deCleyre on the Haymarket martyrs.*

How heavy the heart is now, and every heart
Save only the word drunk, power drunk
Hard capsule of the doomed. How distraught
Those things of pride, the wills nourished in the fat
Years, fed in the kindly twilight of the books
In gold and brown, the voices that had little
To live for, crying for something to die for.
The philosophers of history,
Of dim wit and foolish memory,
The giggling concubines of catastrophe—
Who forget so much—Boethius' calm death,
More's sweet speech, Rosa's broken body—
Or you, tough, stubby recalcitrant
Of Fate.

   Now in Waldheim where the rain
Has fallen careless and unthinking
For all an evil century's youth,
Where now the banks of dark roses lie,
What memory lasts, Emma, of you,
Or of the intrepid comrades of your grave,
Of Piotr, of "mutual aid,"
Against the iron clad flame throwing
Course of time?
    Your stakes were on the turn
Of a card whose face you knew you would not see.

You knew that nothing could ever be
More desperate than truth; and when every voice
Was cowed, you spoke against the coalitions
For the duration of the emergency—
In the permanent emergency
You spoke for the irrefutable
Coalition of the blood of men.

XXIV

Coming back over the col between
Isoceles Mountain and North Palisade,
I stop at the summit and look back
At the storm gathering over the white peaks
Of the Whitney group and the colored
Kaweahs. September, nineteen-thirty-nine.
This is the last trip in the mountains
This autumn, possibly the last trip ever.
The storm clouds rise up the mountainside,
Lightning batters the pinnacles above me,
The clouds beneath the pass are purple
And I see rising through them from the valleys
And cities a cold, murderous flood,
Spreading over the world, lapping at the last
Inviolate heights; mud streaked yellow
With gas, slimy and blotched with crimson,
Filled with broken bits of steel and flesh,
Moving slowly with the blind motion
Of lice, spreading inexorably
As bacteria spread in tissues,
Swirling with the precise rapacity of starved rats.
I loiter here like a condemned man
Lingers over his last breakfast, his last smoke;
Thinking of those heroes of the war
Of human skill, foresight, endurance and will;
The disinterested bravery,
The ideal combat of peace: Bauer
Crawling all night around his icecave
On snowbound Kanchanjunga, Tilman
And Shipton skylarking on Nanda Devi,
Smythe seeing visions on Everest,
The mad children of the Eigerwand—
What holidays will they keep this year?
Gun emplacements blasted in the rock;
No place for graves, the dead covered with quicklime
Or left in the snow till the spring thaw;
Machine gun duels between white robed ski troops,
The last screaming schusses marked with blood.

Was it for this we spent the years perfecting
The craft of courage? Better the corpse
Of the foolhardy, frozen on the Eiger
Accessible only to the storm,
Standing sentry for the avalanche.

XXV

WEDNESDAY OF HOLY WEEK, 1940

Out of the east window a storm
Blooms spasmodically across the moonrise;
In the west, in the haze, the planets
Pulsate like standing meteors.
We listen in the darkness to the service of Tenebrae,
Music older than the Resurrection,
The voice of the ruinous, disorderly Levant:
"Why doth the city sit solitary
That was full of people?"
The voices of the Benedictines are massive, impersonal;
They neither fear this agony nor are ashamed of it.
Think . . . six hours ago in Europe,
Thousands were singing these words,
Putting out the candles psalm by psalm . . .
Albi like a fort in the cold dark,
Aachen, the voices fluttering in the ancient vaulting,
The light of the last candle
In Munich on the gnarled carving.
"Jerusalem, Jerusalem,
Return ye unto the Lord thy God."
Thousands kneeling in the dark,
Saying, "Have mercy upon me O God."
We listen appreciatively, smoking, talking quietly,
The voices are coming from three thousand miles.
On the white garden wall the shadows
Of the date palm thresh wildly;
The full moon of the spring is up,
And a gale with it.

XXVI

ADONIS IN SUMMER

The Lotophagi with their silly hands
Haunt me in sleep, plucking at my sleeve;
Their gibbering laughter and blank eyes
Hide on the edge of the mind's vision
In dusty subways and crowded streets.
Late in August, asleep, Adonis
Appeared to me, frenzied and bleeding
And showed me, clutched in his hand, the plow
That broke the dream of Persephone.
The next day, regarding the scorched grass
In the wilting park, I became aware
That beneath me, beneath the gravel
And the hurrying ants, and the loam
And the subsoil, lay the glacial drift,
The Miocene jungles, the reptiles
Of the Jurassic, the cuttlefish
Of the Devonian, Cambrian
Worms, and the mysteries of the gneiss;
Their histories folded, docketed
In darkness; and deeper still the hot
Black core of iron, and once again
The inscrutable archaic rocks,
And the long geologic ladder,
And the living soil and the strange trees,
And the tangled bodies of lovers
Under the strange stars.
                    And beside me,
A mad old man, plucking at my sleeve.

XXVII

ADONIS IN WINTER

Persephone awaits him in the dim boudoir,
Waits him, for the hour is at hand.
She has arranged the things he likes
Near to his expected hand:
Herrick's poems, tobacco, the juice
Of pomegranates in a twisted glass.
She piles her drugged blonde hair
Above her candid forehead,
Touches up lips and eyelashes,
Selects her most naked robe.
On the stroke of the equinox he comes,
And smiles, and stretches his arms, and strokes
Her cheeks and childish shoulders, and kisses
The violet lids closed on the grey eyes.
Free of aggressive Aphrodite,
Free of the patronizing gods,
The cruel climate of Olympus,
They feed caramels to Cerberus
And warn him not to tell
The cuckold Pluto of their adulteries,
Their mortal lechery in dispassionate Hell.

XXVIII

UN BEL DI VENDREMO

"Hello NBC, this is London speaking. . ."
I move the dial, I have heard it all,
Day after day—the terrible waiting,
The air raids, the military communiqués,
The between the lines whispering
Of quarreling politicians,
The mute courage of the people.
The dial moves over aggressive
Advertisements, comedians, bands hot and sweet,
To a record concert—La Scala—Madame Butterfly.
I pause, listening idly, and suddenly
I feel as though I had begun to fall
Slowly, buoyantly, through infinite, indefinite space.
Milano, fretting in my seat,
In my lace collar and velvet suit,
My beautiful mother weeping
Happily beside me. My God,
How long ago it was, further far
Than Rome or Egypt, that other
World before the other war.
Stealing downstairs to spy on the champagne suppers;
Watching the blue flame of the chafing dish
On Sunday nights; driving over middle Europe
Behind a café au lait team,
The evenings misty, smelling of cattle
And the fat Danubian earth.
It will never be again
The open work stockings,
The lace evening gowns,
The pink roses on the slippers;
Debs eating roast chicken and drinking whiskey,
On the front porch with grandpa;
The neighbors gaping behind their curtains;
The Japanese prints and the works of Huneker.
Never again will a small boy
Curled in the hammock in the murmurous summer air,
Gnaw his knuckles, reading *The Jungle;*

Never again will he gasp as Franz Joseph
And the princesses sweep through
The lines of wolf caped hussars.
It is a terrible thing to sit here
In the uneasy light above this strange city
And listen to the poignant sentimentality
Of an age more dead than the Cro Magnon.
It is a terrible thing to see a world die twice,
"The first time as tragedy,
The second as evil farce."

XXIX

ANDREE REXROTH

Purple and green, blue and white,
The Oregon river mouths
Slide into thick smoky darkness
As the turning cup of day
Slips from the whirling hemisphere.
And all that white long beach gleams
In white twilight as the lights
Come on in the lonely hamlets;
And voices of men emerge;
And dogs barking, as the wind stills.
Those August evenings are
Sixteen years old tonight and I
Am sixteen years older too—
Lonely, caught in the midst of life,
In the chaos of the world;
And all the years that we were young
Are gone, and every atom
Of your learned and disordered
Flesh is utterly consumed.

XXX

Climbing alone all day long
In the blazing waste of spring snow,
I came down with the sunset's edge
To the highest meadow, green
In the cold mist of waterfalls,
To a cobweb of water
Woven with innumerable
Bright flowers of wild iris;
And saw far down our fire's smoke
Rising between the canyon walls,
A human thing in the empty mountains.
And as I stood on the stones
In the midst of whirling water,
The whirling iris perfume
Caught me in a vision of you
More real than reality:
Fire in the deep curves of your hair;
Your hips whirled in a tango,
Out and back in dim scented light;
Your cheeks snow-flushed, the zithers
Ringing, all the crowded ski lodge
Dancing and singing; your arms
White in the brown autumn water,
Swimming through the fallen leaves,
Making a fluctuant cobweb
Of light on the sycamores;
Your thigh's exact curve, the fine gauze
Slipping through my hands, and you
Tense on the verge of abandon;
Your breasts' very touch and smell;
The sweet secret odor of sex.
Forever the thought of you,
And the splendor of the iris,
The crinkled iris petal,
The gold hairs powdered with pollen,
And the obscure cantata
Of the tangled water, and the
Burning, impassive snow peaks,
Are knotted together here.

This moment of fact and vision
Seizes immortality,
Becomes the person of this place.
The responsibility
Of love realized and beauty
Seen burns in a burning angel
Real beyond flower or stone.

XXXI

HARMODIUS AND ARISTOGEITON

Last night, reading the Anthology,
I could find no epitaph for you.
I suppose it was naive to look.
Alexander and Justinian,
The brocaded Paleologoi,
French drunkards and sleepy Turks,
Have ruled over Athens since your day.
So, late by these many years, take this:

Your act is vocal still. Men grow deaf.

XXXII

Her boudoir is ornamented with
The works of the Bloomsbury mystics—
Limited editions in warped vellum;
There is also a mauve draped pric-dieu
And a New Mexican crucifix.
Sinister and intimidating
As this environment might appear,
Her ecstasies can be distinguished
From those of Lais the agnostic
Only by their singular frequency.

XXXIII

I know your moral sources, prig.
Last night you plunged awake screaming.
You dreamed you'd grown extremely old,
Lay dying, and to your deathbed,
All the girls you'd ever slept with
Came, as old as you, to watch you die.
Comatose, your blotched residues
Shrivelled and froze between stiff sheets;
And the faces, dim as under
Dirty water, incurious,
Silent, of a room full of old,
Old women, waited, patiently.

XXXIV

Septimius, the forms you know so well,
The olla of callas, the multiform
Guitar, the svelt girl torso and slick thigh,
Surprise you and become you unaware.
You get drunk like one of your spotless nudes;
I hear that you resemble a still life
Between sheets; and your conversation ticks
From certitude to tock;
But not with me.

XXXV

I have long desired to shine
As the modern Juvenal.
However, when I survey
The vast jungle infested
With bushmasters and tsetse
Flies imperviously stretched
From A . . . . . S . . . . to C . . . . . .
H . . . . F . . . , from M . . . . .
D . . . . . to L . . . M . . . . . ,
I resign myself perforce
To Martial's brief excursions.

XXXVI

Think, as we lie in this sweet bed,
With the lamplight dim on books
And pictures of three thousand years,
And the light caught in the wine
Like Mars or Aldebaran:
Vaulted over the winter mountains,
The night sky is like the pure
Space of the imagination—
Defined by infinite star points,
Interrupted by meteors,
And the fleshy fires of planets
That move like infusoria.
The moon is as sheer as glass;
Its globe dissolves in illusion;
Out from it flow mysterious
Lines and surfaces, folding
And unfolding without limit.
The Carmina Burana—
Differential geometry—
"Dum Dianae vitrea
While Diana's crystal lamp"
Proof of the questionable
Existence of integrals—
And this bloody sacrament,
This linking of corpuscles
Like atoms of oxygen,
This Matrimony called Holy,
This is the lens of intention,
Focusing liability
From world to person, from passion
To action; and conversely,
The source of potential in fact.
The individual—the world—
On the bookshelves there is only
Paper soiled by history.
The space of night is infinite,
The blackness and emptiness
Crossed only by thin bright fences
Of logic.

Lying under
The night sky's inexhaustible
Equation, and fallen from it,
Uncountable hexagons
Of snow blanket the streamlined
Volcanic stones, and the columns
Of hexagonal basalt,
And the hexagons of wax
And honey where the bees sleep.

XXXVII

Autumn has returned and we return
To the same beach in the last hours.
The Phoenix and the Tortoise is finished.
The gratuitous discipline of finality
Falls on our lives and shapes our ends.
Ourselves as objectives, our objects,
Pass from our hands to the hands of time.
Reconsidering and revising
My life and the meaning of my poem,
I gather once more within me
The old material, sea and stone.

The green spring that comes in November
With the first rains has restored the hills.
Seals are playing in the kelp beds.
As the surf sweeps in they can be seen
Weaving over one another in
The standing water. In the granite
Cliffs are swarms of dark fish shaped patches
Of rock oriented to the flow lines
Of the hot magma. Nobody knows
Exactly what caused their formation,
Deep in the blind earth under the blind
Jurassic world, under the dead
Franciscan series, what disorder,
What process. On the wet sand lie
Hundreds of jellyfish with pale
Lavender organs at their hearts.
The sun will dry them and leave only
A brittle film. There are more hundreds
Pulsing through the water, struggling
Against the drive of the rising tide.
Down the beach beyond a tangle
Of barbed wire an armed sentry stands,
Gazing seaward under his helmet.

Carapace or transfiguration—
History will doubtless permit us
Neither. Eventually the will

81

Exhausts itself and turns, seeking grace,
To the love that suffers ignorance
And time's irresponsibility.
The Cross cannot be climbed upon.
It cannot be seized like a weapon
Against the injustice of the world.
"No one has ever seized injustice
In his bare hands and bent it back.
No one has ever tried to smash evil,
Without smashing himself and sinking
Into greater evil or despair."
The Satanic cunning represents
Itself as very strong, but just
A trifle weaker than its victim.
This is the meaning of temptation.
The Devil does not fool with fools.

It is easy to read or write
In a book, "Self realization
Is responsible self sacrifice."
"The will to power, the will to live,
Are fulfilled by transfiguration."
"The person is the final value;
Value is responsibility."
As the world sinks in a marsh of blood,
You won't raise yourself by your bootstraps,
However pious and profound.
Christ was not born of Socrates,
But to a disorderly people,
In an evil time, in the flesh
Of innocence and humility.

"The self determining will." What self?
What determination? History
Plays its pieces—"The Japanese
Adventure was shaped on the countless
G'oto tables of a hundred years."

Black slowly immobilizes white.
Evil reveals its hidden aces.
As the Philosopher observes,

"Fear is the sentiment of men
Beaten and overcome in mind,
Confronted by an imminent evil
Which they take to be too much for them
To resist and more than they can bear."
And again, appropriately, in the Rhetoric,
"We are never afraid of evil
When we are in the thick of it
And all chance of escape has vanished.
Fear always looks to flight, and catches
With the fancy's eye some glimpse
Of an opening for the avoidance
Of evil."

       "O my Father, all things
Are possible unto Thee, if it be
Possible let this cup pass from me.
Nevertheless, not my will, but Thine."

The self determining will accepts
The responsibility of all
Contingency. What will? What self?
The Cross descends into the world
Like a sword, but the hilt thereof
Is in the heavens. Every man
Is his own Adam, left to itself,
The self unselfs itself, the will
Demands autonomy and achieves
It by a system of strategic
Retreats—the inane autonomy
Of the morally neuter event.
Conversion, penitence, and grace—
Autonomy is a by product
Of identification.

What was our sacrifice worth?
Practically nothing, the waste
Of time overwhelms heroes,
Pyramids and catastrophes.
Who knows the tropical foci
Of the Jurassic ice flows?

Who has seen the frozen black mass
That rushes upon us biding
Its light years? Who remembers
The squad that died stopping the tanks
At the bridgehead? The company
Was bombed out an hour later.
Simonides is soon forgotten.
The pressure of the unfound
Future is the pressure of the lost
Past, the brain stiffens with hope,
And swims in hallucination
Beating its spinal column
Like a flagellate in a mild
Solution of alcohol,
And pressed against it, mantis
To mantis, the cobwebbed body—
The caput abdominale.
As for that thin entelechy,
The person, let him wear the head
Of the wolf, in Sherwood Forest.

We return? Each to each, one
To another, each to the other?
Sweet lovely hallucination—
The sea falls through you, through the gulf
Of wish—last spring—what was value?
The hole itself cuts in its self
And watches as it fills with blood?
The waves of the sea fall through
Our each others indomitable
As peristalsis.

      Autumn comes
And the death of flowers, but
The flowered colored waves of
The sea will last forever
Like the pattern on the dress
Of a beautiful woman.

Nineteen forty-two and we
Are selves, stained, fixed and mounted

On the calendar—and the leaves
  Fall easily in the gardens
Of a million ruins.

      And deep
In the mountains the wind has stopped
The current of a stream with only
A windrow of the terribly
Red dogwood leaves.

·III·

TRANSLATIONS AND IMITATIONS

RUMOR LAETALIS

I am constantly wounded
By the deadly gossip that adds
Insult to injury, that
Punishes me mercilessly
With the news of your latest
Scandal in my ears. Wherever
I go the smirking fame of each
Fresh despicable infamy
Has run on ahead of me.
Can't you learn to be cautious
About your lecheries?
Hide your practices in darkness;
Keep away from raised eyebrows.
If you must murder love, do it
Covertly, with your candied
Prurience and murmured lewdness.

You were never the heroine
Of dirty stories in the days
When love bound us together.
Now those links are broken, desire
Is frozen, and you are free
To indulge every morbid lust,
And filthy jokes about your
Latest amour are the delight
Of every cocktail party.
Your boudoir is a brothel;
Your salon is a saloon;
Even your sensibilities
And your depraved innocence
Are only special premiums,
Rewards of a shameful commerce.

O the heart breaking memory
Of days like flowers, and your
Eyes that shone like Venus the star
In our brief nights, and the soft bird
Flight of your love about me;
And now your eyes are as bitter

As a rattlesnake's dead eyes,
And your disdain as malignant.
Those who give off the smell of coin
You warm in bed; I who have
Love to bring am not even
Allowed to speak to you now.
You receive charlatans and fools;
I have only the swindling
Memory of poisoned honey.

—*Carmina Burana*
[*Abælard?*]

The city is silent;
Sound drains away;
Buildings vanish in the light of dawn;
Cold sunlight comes on the highest peak;
The thick dust of night
Clings to the hills;
The earth opens;
The river boats are vague;
The still sky—
The sound of falling leaves.
A huge doe comes to the garden gate,
Lost from the herd,
Seeking its fellows.
                              —*Tu Fu*

⊕

Here we part.
You go off in the distance,
And once more the forested mountains
Are empty, unfriendly.
What holiday will see us
Drunk together again?
Last night we walked
Arm in arm in the moonlight,
Singing sentimental ballads
Along the banks of the river.
Your honor outlasts three emperors.
I go back to my lonely house by the river,
Mute, friendless, feeding the crumbling years.

                              —*Tu Fu*

It is late in the year;
Yin and Yang struggle
In the brief sunlight.
On the desert mountains
Frost and snow
Gleam in the freezing night.
Past midnight,
Drums and bugles ring out,
Violent, cutting the heart.
Over the Triple Gorge the Milky Way
Pulsates between the stars.
The bitter cries of thousands of households
Can be heard above the noise of battle.
Everywhere the workers sing wild songs.
The great heroes and generals of old time
Are yellow dust forever now.
Such are the affairs of men.
Poetry and letters
Persist in silence and solitude.

—*Tu Fu*

Zonas

Pass me the sweet earthenware jug,
Made of the earth that bore me,
The earth that someday I shall bear.

❀

Anonymous
Epitaph of Sardanapallus

I keep the taste of feasting,
And the wage of wantonness,
And the joys shared with lovers;
But the blessings of many
Possessions I leave behind.

❀

Marcus Argentarius

Dead, they'll burn you up with electricity,
An interesting experience,
But quite briefly illuminating—
So pour the whiskey and kiss my wife or yours,
And I'll reciprocate. Stop fretting your brains.
In Hell the learned sit in long rows saying,
"Some A-s are not B-s, there exists a not B."
You'll have time to grow wise in their company.

93

Antipater of Sidon

Fortune tellers say I won't last long;
It looks like it from the newspapers;
But there is better conversation
In Hell than in an insane nation;
And a galloping jug will get there
Quicker than these loud pedestrians,
Tumbling down hill witless in the dust.

❀

Antipater of Thessalonica

Neither war, nor cyclones, nor earthquakes,
Are as terrifying as this oaf,
Who stares, sips water, and remembers
Everything we say.

❀

Several Sources

I know I am poor,
Neither do I have to be reminded
Of my own name or
The day of the week.
All your bitterness will get us nowhere.
Wash the anchovies,
While I pour the wine.
Naked and drunk, we'll find riches in bed.

Anonymous

Flowers will do us no good on our tombstones;
Tears mixed with ashes only make mud.
Let's move half the garden into the bedroom,
Roll about, and moan in unison.

❀

Philodemus

Herakles' rebuttal was too much
For the thug who butted folks to death.
Your sophisticated responses
Have left me crippled, on the near side
Of middle age and midnight.

❀

Meleager

What have you got to crow about,
Beating yourself with your red wings?
This hour is for final drowsy
Wantonries, not for your noisy
Virility. Go back to bed,
Or we will mourn this maidenhead
With a chicken dinner.

Sthenelais—Anonymous

The latest incendiary flesh,
That gorgeous exorbitant strumpet
Whose very farts are marketed by Troy weight,
Bedded bare with me for a night long
Thoroughly unsymbolical dream—
And every caper gratis. I am finished
Genuflecting for you, you sadist—
Asleep, I play marbles with emeralds.

❁

Martial

Since your marriage you have lost the look
Of a morose, inhibited wolf.
Perhaps your wife is reversible?

❁

Martial
[*To a Revolutionary Surrealist*]

Don't pay any attention
To this synthetic spectre
Raving interchangeably
About the revolution
Of the exploited masses
And the diseased gyrations
Of his sensibilities.
He was a bride last night.

Ausonius, after Rufinus

I used to tell you, "Frances, we grow old.
The years fly away. Don't be so private
With those parts. A chaste maid is an old maid."
Unnoticed by your disdain, old age crept
Close to us. Those days are gone past recall.
And now you come, penitent and crying
Over your old lack of courage, over
Your present lack of beauty. It's all right.
Closed in your arms, we'll share our smashed delights.
It's give and take now. It's what I wanted,
If not what I want.

※

Paulus Silentiarius

Don't tell me I'm getting gray,
That my eyes are red and bleared.
It's just love having a romp.
He kicks me where it hurts most,
Sticks arrows in me for fun,
Keeps me awake with lewd tales;
My loins are prematurely
Shrivelled; my neck is scrawny;
I wane in a waxing fire.
If you would only relent—
I would grow plump at your touch,
And my hair turn black in a night.

Meleager

Down through the earth as a last gift,
Heliodora, I send you
My tears—tears of pain on a tomb
Already wet with weeping.
There was a time I wept for love
Longed for and love satisfied; now
I have only pain of love lost—
An empty gift to send you, dead.
O God, you were so beautiful,
So desirable. Death seized you,
Violated you like a flower
Smashed into dust. Let the earth
Which has borne us all, bear you,
Mourned by all, gently forever.

❁

Tymnes

Eumelus had a Maltese dog.
He called him Bull. He was the most
Loyal dog that ever lived.
His bark comes faintly up from Hell,
Lost on the night bound roads.

Secundus of Tarentum
  —after Plato.

I Lais, once an arrow
In the heart of all, am Lais
No longer, but a witness
To the harrying of the years.
I swear by Desire, (and what
Is Desire now but a swearword?)
Lais can no longer see
Lais in Lais herself.

❁

Leonidas of Tarentum

Here is Clito's little shack.
Here is his little cornpatch.
Here is his tiny vineyard.
Here is his little woodlot.
Here Clito spent eighty years.

❁

Leonidas of Tarentum

By themselves in the twilight
The cattle came home
Over the snow drifted hill.
Profoundly asleep,
The cowboy lies by an oak,
Stricken by lightning.

Sulpicius Lupercus Servasius, Jr.

Rivers level granite mountains,
Rains wash the figures from the sundial,
The plowshare wears thin in the furrow;
And on the fingers of the mighty,
The gold of authority is bright
With the glitter of attrition.

❁

Anonymous

Splendid ingenuity
Went to the manufacture
Of the water ousel's nest
Hung beneath the waterfall.
It is built for a season.

❁

Crates

Time's fingers bend us slowly
With dubious craftsmanship,
That at last spoils all it forms.